Facing Mighty Fears
About Making Mistakes

Dr. Dawn's Mini Books About Mighty Fears
By Dawn Huebner, PhD
Illustrated by Liza Stevens
Helping children ages 6–10 live happier lives

Facing Mighty Fears
About Animals
ISBN 978 1 78775 946 6
eISBN 978 1 78775 947 3

Facing Mighty Fears About
Baddies and Villains
ISBN 978 1 83997 462 5
eISBN 978 1 83997 463 2

Facing Mighty Fears
About Health
ISBN 978 1 78775 928 2
eISBN 978 1 78775 927 5

Facing Mighty Fears
About Throwing Up
ISBN 978 1 78775 925 1
eISBN 978 1 78775 926 8

Facing Mighty Fears
About Trying New Things
ISBN 978 1 78775 950 3
eISBN 978 1 78775 951 0

Watch for future titles in the
*Dr. Dawn's Mini Books About
Mighty Fears* series.

Facing Mighty Fears About Making Mistakes

Dawn Huebner, PhD

Illustrated by Liza Stevens

Jessica Kingsley Publishers
London and Philadelphia

First published in Great Britain in 2023 by Jessica Kingsley Publishers
An imprint of John Murray Press

1

A CIP catalogue record for this title is available from the
British Library and the Library of Congress

ISBN 978 1 83997 466 3
eISBN 978 1 83997 467 0

Printed and bound in Great Britain by TJ Books Limited

Jessica Kingsley Publishers' policy is to use papers that are natural,
renewable, and recyclable products and made from wood grown in
sustainable forests. The logging and manufacturing processes are expected
to conform to the environmental regulations of the country of origin.

Jessica Kingsley Publishers
Carmelite House
50 Victoria Embankment
London EC4Y 0DZ

www.jkp.com

John Murray Press
Part of Hodder & Stoughton Limited
An Hachette UK Company

MIX
Paper from
responsible sources
FSC® C013056

Grown-ups:

Need ideas about how to use this book?

Please see Dr. Dawn's
Note to Parents and Caregivers
on page 69.

You'll also find a **Resource Section**
highlighting books, websites, and organizations
for parents of anxious kids.

If you have ever been around a newborn, you know there is not much they can do.

Tiny babies can't sit up, or roll over, or clap their hands.

They can't tie their shoes, or kick a ball, or eat with a fork, or answer questions, even easy ones.

When you were a baby, you couldn't do those things, either.

And then, over time, you learned.

FUN FACT
Albert Einstein, one of the most brilliant physicists of all time, didn't speak until he was 4 years old and couldn't read until he was 7.

How did that happen?

How did you go from being a baby who knew so little to the clever, capable person you are today?

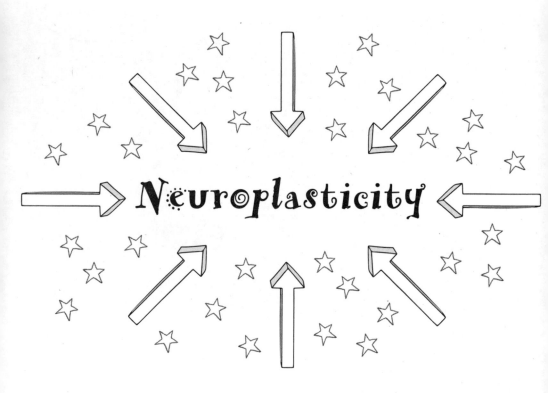

Neuroplasticity

Neuroplasticity is your brain's ability to grow, and change, and learn.

But how, exactly, does it work?

When you were born, your brain was crammed full of tiny cells called neurons. Billions of them.

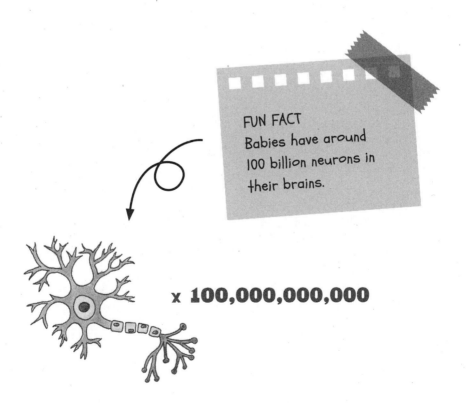

FUN FACT
Babies have around 100 billion neurons in their brains.

x **100,000,000,000**

Neurons are like little electrical wires, ready to carry messages from one place to another.

When one neuron carries a message to another neuron, the two get linked together, making a pathway in your brain.

Eventually, millions of neurons get linked, creating a complex web of crisscrossing paths.

Brushing your teeth, remembering the words to a song, hitting a tennis ball, saying please when you want something, buckling your seatbelt as soon as you get into a car—each skill exists in your brain as a pathway.

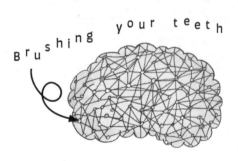

New brain paths form each time you learn or do something for the first time.

But brain paths are weak at the start.

If they don't get used, they fade away.

It works this way for everyone.

The smartest, most talented people you know started with a jumble of disconnected neurons, just like you.

They worked to link their neurons together, just like you.

FUN FACT
Professional athletes practice 6-8 hours a day most days of the week.

And then, importantly, they practiced, because working at something strengthens neural pathways and helps them run more smoothly.

Being good at something right away has nothing to do with it.

In fact, taking on challenges and doing things you *aren't* very good at is one of the best ways to keep your brain web healthy and strong.

FUN FACT
Thomas Edison tried 1,000 times before successfully creating a glass bulb that lit up. When asked how all those failures felt, Edison said he hadn't failed a thousand times. In his view, he had figured out what didn't work on his way to discovering what did. His attitude and stick-to-it-iveness led to the invention of the lightbulb.

FUN FACT
Thomas Edison also said that many of life's failures come from people who give up without realizing how close they are to succeeding.

That means that you can mess up, and fumble, and fail. In fact, you should do these things. Mistakes are exactly what your brain needs to grow.

Some kids hate making mistakes.

They get **angry** if they aren't immediately good at something and avoid taking on challenges because messing up even a little makes them feel bad about themselves.

These kids often compare themselves to other people and insist on being

first,

best,

fastest,

the winner

all the time.

It's hard to live that way.

And actually, it isn't as good for your brain.

So, the key to having a healthy brain and feeling happy more often is to get used to messing up, and coming in second, and getting things wrong.

To know that mistakes are part of learning, and don't mean anything bad about you.

FUN FACT
Orville and Wilbur Wright worked on a flying machine for 4 years, modifying the design after every crash until, in 1903, it was able to stay in the air for almost a minute. Wahoo! But they knew they needed to do better. The perseverance of these two brothers is why we are able to fly long distances today.

FUN FACT
It took Sir James Dyson 5,126 tries to get a properly working vacuum cleaner. His brand is now worth billions of dollars.

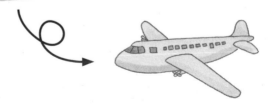

You can do that.

You can learn how to be okay with mistakes.

All you have to do is create a new brain path.

The following 4 steps can help.

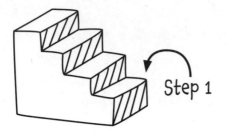

Step 1

1. Say oops.

There's a saying:

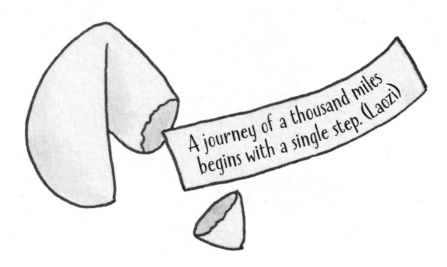

A journey of a thousand miles begins with a single step. (Laozi)

That means that no matter how hard something is, how impossible it may seem, one small step is enough to get you started.

The first step on the path to being okay with mistakes is to decide on a word.

Your word can be real or made up.

Long or short.

Funny or serious.

Choose a word you like, though, one that feels good in your mouth, because you are going to say this word whenever you make a mistake.

FUN FACT
Pro basketball player Michael Jordan was cut from his high school basketball team.

FUN FACT
This same Michael Jordan, now one of the world's most famous basketball players, later said, "I have missed more than 9,000 shots in my career. I have lost almost 300 games. On 26 occasions I have been entrusted to take the game-winning shot, and I missed. I have failed over and over again, and that is why I succeed."

Fiddlesticks!

When luck goes against you. When you are losing a game, or don't get picked for a team.

Nerts

FUN FACT
Before becoming a famous singer, Madonna worked at a donut store, although she lasted just one day. She was fired for mistakenly squirting jelly filling on a customer.

FUN FACT
In 1993, the now famous singer, Beyoncé, lost on a television talent show.

FUN FACT
Dr. Seuss, author of The Cat in the Hat and many other books, was rejected by 27 publishers. Feeling discouraged, he was on his way home to burn his latest manuscript when he ran into an old school friend, who happened to be a publisher. His books went on to sell millions of copies, including the book he was about to burn.

Drat!

When someone corrects you.

When something you thought would be easy turns out to be hard.

FUN FACT
Colonel Sanders was told "no" by 1,009 restaurant owners before one agreed to his idea, now known as Kentucky Fried Chicken.

FUN FACT
Vincent Van Gogh struggled to make it as an artist, selling only one painting in his entire life, although his paintings now hang in famous museums and sell for millions of dollars.

Oof

Ask your family to help.

Everyone can use the same word, or each person can pick a word of their own.

And then every time a mistake happens, or someone loses, or things go wrong:

That's it. One step. And your journey to being okay
with mistakes has begun.

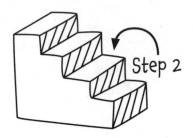

Step 2

2. Breathe.

Step 2 has to do with a small part of your brain called the amygdala.

The amygdala is always on the lookout for danger.

When this part of your brain picks up on something that might be a problem, it sounds an alarm.

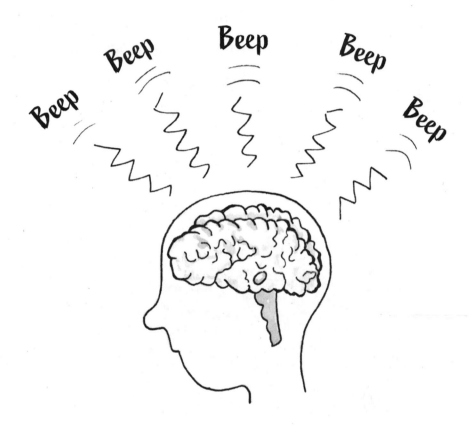

The fact that your amygdala alerts you to danger is great.

You need to have a part of your brain working to keep you safe.

FUN FACT

A vendor at the 1904 World's Fair ran out of bowls for the ice cream he was selling. Not wanting the rest of his ice cream to go to waste, he agreed when the vendor next to him suggested curling the waffles he was selling into cones. The creativity and flexibility of these two food-sellers is why we have ice cream cones today.

There's just one small problem: your amygdala isn't always right.

It sometimes sounds an alarm when there is no danger, or when there is a problem, but it's one you can handle.

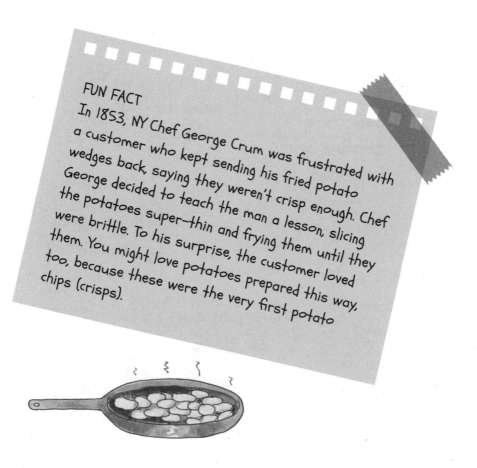

FUN FACT

In 1853, NY Chef George Crum was frustrated with a customer who kept sending his fried potato wedges back, saying they weren't crisp enough. Chef George decided to teach the man a lesson, slicing the potatoes super-thin and frying them until they were brittle. To his surprise, the customer loved them. You might love potatoes prepared this way, too, because these were the very first potato chips (crisps).

That's what's been happening in your brain.

When you feel unsure of yourself, or make a mistake, or struggle to understand something, your amygdala has been sounding an alarm.

And the alarm makes you think:

Your brain alarm, and the negative thoughts that follow, make you feel

sad

MAD

frustrated

stupid

hopeless

tearful

discouraged

and other unpleasant things.

The grown-ups around you might notice you getting upset and try to cheer you up, saying things like:

But when you are upset, you can't hear these things because your brain alarm is clanging too loudly.

So, before anyone tries to reason with you, or reassure you, or get you to see things differently, you need to quiet your amygdala. And the best way to do that is to breathe.

There are lots of breathing methods. Try a few to see which you like best.

Balloon Breaths

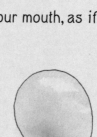

1. Sit comfortably.

2. Cup your hands around your mouth.

3. Take a deep breath in through your nose.

4. Blow slowly but forcefully out through your mouth, as if you were blowing up a balloon.

5. Gradually expand your hands, like an imaginary balloon filling up.

6. Take another breath in through your nose and repeat, moving your hands further out to show the balloon getting bigger.

7. Blow up several balloons.

Lemon Squeeze Breaths

1. Sit comfortably.

2. Imagine you are holding a lemon in each hand.

3. Breathe in through your nose while squeezing both hands—as if you were trying to get all the juice out of your imaginary lemons.

4. Hold your breath—and the squeeze—while you count to 3 in your head.

5. Release your hands and breathe out long and slow.

6. Repeat 3 times.

Color Breaths

1. Sit comfortably.

2. Picture a calm, happy color, one that makes you feel good inside.

3. Take a deep breath in through your nose, pulling that color into your body.

4. Briefly hold your breath as you think of a color that reminds you of anger or stress.

5. Breathe out slowly through your mouth, imagining the stressful color leaving your body.

6. Repeat 3 times.

If you don't like any of these methods, go online to look for breathing and mindfulness activities for kids. There are all sorts of apps and videos and books that can teach you to quiet your brain.

(Psst: That's because everyone needs to do it, not just you.)

When you find the method you like best,
practice it.

Practice first when you *aren't* upset. Even two or
three minutes of calm breathing will get a new
pathway going in your brain.

And then, when you are losing a game, or you make
a mistake, or you try something that turns out to be
difficult, do your first two steps:

1. Say your special word.

2. B-r-e-a-t-h-e.

And you will be on your way.

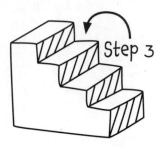

3. Self-talk.

Did you know that we all talk to ourselves? This is called—drumroll please—self-talk.

Self-talk can be:

POSITIVE which means we say helpful things to ourselves

or

NEGATIVE which means we say unhelpful things.

Kids who hate making mistakes have lots of negative self-talk.

If you think things like this, it isn't your fault.

Negative thoughts have a way of bubbling up, and you can't just put up your hands to stop them.

You can't prevent negative thoughts, but you can recognize them for what they are: just thoughts, nothing more.

Then, say something positive to yourself like:

Saying these things might feel strange at first.

You are used to your negative self-talk.

But you can get used to positive self-talk, too.

FUN FACT
In 1928, Sir Alexander Fleming was trying to find a cure for influenza (the flu), but his experiment wasn't working. Frustrated, he dumped everything in the garbage and left for a holiday. When he returned two weeks later, he noticed that the mold on one of the petri dishes in the garbage was dissolving the bacteria around it. What seemed like a failed experiment led to the discovery of penicillin, still one of our most powerful antibiotics. When asked about his discovery, Fleming said, "One sometimes finds what one is not looking for."

FUN FACT
Engineers Alfred Fielding and Marc Chavannes designed textured wallpaper, but it was a flop. Not sure what to do with the long plastic sheets sporting air bubbles meant to hang on a wall, they used it to wrap packages instead. Eureka! Bubble wrap!

FUN FACT
Abraham Lincoln lost many elections before running for President of the United States and winning. Most famous for ending slavery in America, Lincoln said, "Success is going from failure to failure without losing your enthusiasm."

Look at the positive sentences again.

Mistakes make my brain grow.

I can't do this yet.

I was born to learn.

I'm on the right track.

I can do hard things.

Learning is my superpower.

Write down the sentences you like best or make up a few of your own.

Then, when you make a mistake, read one of your positive sentences.

Mistakes make my brain grow.

I can do hard things.

When you lose a game, think of one of your sentences.

When someone corrects you or tries to teach you something, think of one of your sentences.

When you are doing something that doesn't come easily to you, think of one of your sentences.

FUN FACT

Ruth Wakefield ran out of the baker's chocolate she needed to make cookies. She decided to break off bits of a different kind of chocolate to see if they would melt into the dough. They didn't. The small bits of chocolate suspended in the dough looked odd, but she decided to try a cookie anyway. Voila! The chocolate chip cookie was born.

I was born to learn.

Learning is my superpower.

I can do hard things.

FUN FACT

Comedian Jerry Seinfeld froze his first time on stage, completely forgetting his lines. He was laughed at and booed, but he didn't give up. He went back the next night, and the next, eventually creating the show Seinfeld, described as one of the greatest shows of all time.

I can't do this yet.

Soon you will see that all this positive self-talk makes you feel **happy, energized, hopeful, interested, curious, capable, calm, and proud.**

FUN FACT
Play-Doh was invented in Ohio in 1956 as a way to clean wallpaper, but it didn't work. As the company was going out of business, a preschool teacher commented that the putty was fun to squish. She was right! Play-Doh is now one of the most popular toys in the world.

Mistakes make my brain grow.

FUN FACT
Unable to get recording companies to notice him, rapper Jay-Z started his career selling CDs of his music from the trunk of his car.

I'm on the right track.

Good for you!

You have helped yourself feel better by changing your self-talk.

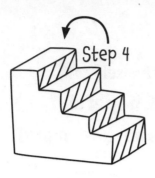

4. Practice making mistakes.

Remember we talked about brain paths being weak at the start?

They get formed easily but if they don't get used, they fade away.

That's why grown-ups are always so keen on practice.

Your parents and teachers probably ask you to practice lots of things.

reading

spelling

dance

math

basketball

Piano

saying please

being nice to your siblings

helping around the house

chewing with your mouth closed

swimming

flossing

recorder

handwriting

history facts

But there's one thing they probably don't ask you to practice:

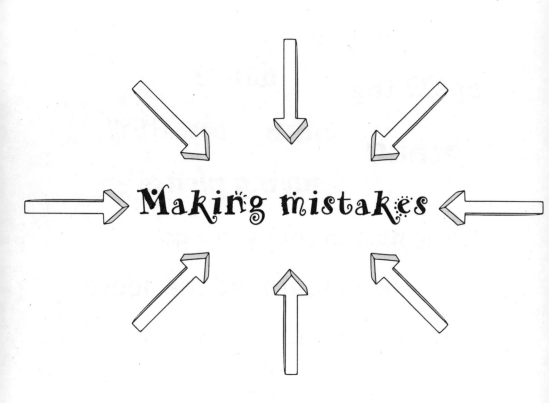

Making mistakes

And yet, that is exactly what you need to do.

You're kidding?!

What?

Huh?

That's right.

To get to the point of being okay with mistakes, you need to practice making them.

On purpose.

Every day.

Making mistakes on purpose allows you to practice responding calmly.

And it shows you that making mistakes, and losing, and having to work hard at something, doesn't mean anything bad about you.

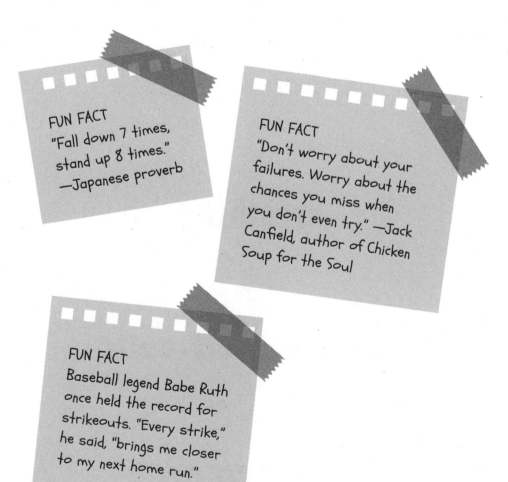

FUN FACT
"Fall down 7 times, stand up 8 times."
—Japanese proverb

FUN FACT
"Don't worry about your failures. Worry about the chances you miss when you don't even try." —Jack Canfield, author of Chicken Soup for the Soul

FUN FACT
Baseball legend Babe Ruth once held the record for strikeouts. "Every strike," he said, "brings me closer to my next home run."

Practicing making mistakes (on purpose) helps you create a new brain path, one that goes like this:

MISTAKE

special word

breathing

positive self-talk

MOVING ON

If you practice making mistakes enough, this new brain path will become the path you naturally follow, the one that feels best to you.

So, this is your fourth step: practice making mistakes. And do your other 3 steps every time.

You might be wondering, "Wait. How do I make a mistake on purpose?"

It's easy. You can:

→ Color outside the lines.

→ Write a letter backwards.

→ Miss a catch.

→ Spill something.

→ Give the wrong answer to a question you know
the answer to.

→ Misspell a word and leave it that way.

→ Get a math problem wrong.

→ Ask an obvious question.

Challenge yourself to make more and more mistakes.

You can make one mistake the first day, two the second day, three the third day, five the fourth day because—you guessed it—that would be a mistake.

You can roll a die at the start of the day and whatever number comes up, that's the number of mistakes you will make that day.

Or you can have a mistake contest in your family, to see who can make the most.

CHAMPION
MISTAKE-MAKER

That's it. Just 4 steps:

1. Say your word.

2. Breathe.

3. Use positive self-talk.

4. Practice making mistakes.

When you do all 4 steps, you will see that mistakes are not such a big deal.

You can make them and get past them.

And then you can get on with your life.

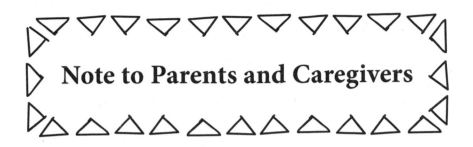

Note to Parents and Caregivers

Persistence. Grit. Stick-to-it-iveness. Determination. Doggedness. Stamina. Tenacity. Resolve. Diligence. Dedication. Steadfastness. Indefatigability. Pluck. Perseverance. Endurance. Will. Toughness. Mettle. Indomitability. Moxie.

Whatever word you use, you undoubtedly want your child to develop this important skill. To work hard and hang in there when the going gets tough. But many children have trouble with this skill, getting angry when there is a hiccup. Or crumbling. Or refusing to even try.

Children who lack stick-to-it-iveness see challenges as insurmountable. They assume there is something wrong with them, or wrong with the task, and they give up. "I don't like that. It's boring" is a common refrain, as is the assertion that they aren't smart enough, fast enough, good enough and, importantly, that this will never change. These children have what is referred to as a fixed mindset, believing they are either good at something or bad at it. Period. End of sentence.

Psychologist Carol Dweck describes the alternative to this fixed mindset as a growth mindset. Children with a growth mindset recognize that mistakes are part of learning, and that challenge is an opportunity to try something new. These children do better on all sorts of measures having to do with academic achievement, social competence, happiness, and even health. It turns out that doing hard things—trying and failing and trying again—is exactly what we need to have brains that are healthy and strong.

That's why it's important to make "We do hard things" part of your family's ethos. And to not only normalize—but also celebrate—mistakes and struggle. This book can help.

Read *Facing Mighty Fears About Making Mistakes* with your child. Go slowly, pausing to enjoy the Fun Facts highlighting the ubiquity of, and hidden benefits to, messing up. Encourage your child to do the 4 steps. Better yet, do them together, keeping in mind that many people spend their lives linking self-worth with achievement, a trap you may have unwittingly fallen into. So, use these skills along with your child, modeling a new way of dealing with imperfection. If you find implementation difficult, consider consulting with a therapist able to guide you and your child on this important journey.

Some additional tips

1. Praise effort, hard work, progress, and persistence rather than ease or talent. When your child gets a good grade, for example, rather than, "You're a champion speller!" say something along the lines of, "Well done! You really studied those words."

2. Remember that the more we resist or try to stomp out a feeling, the more it holds on. So rather than trying to "fix" difficult feelings, empathize with your child's frustration, disappointment, embarrassment, or sadness. Help them feel

seen, heard, and understood: "It's hard to not get the knack of it right away." "You've tried and tried, and it still isn't working. That's frustrating!" "This is tricky business. No wonder you are starting to get discouraged." Lead with empathy and stick with it until your child begins to settle down.

3. As your child begins to calm down, provide encouragement along the lines of: "I know you are up to the challenge." "You can do hard things." "I'm proud of you for hanging in there." A vote of confidence, given sincerely, will help your child learn to hang in there.

4. Remember the power of "yet." This simple word reminds your child that struggle is normal and mastery within reach, "You haven't memorized all the words yet." "You're not able to do 20 sit-ups yet." "You're still working on it. That's okay."

5. Help your child see that there is a learning curve. Being a beginner means not knowing things, or not being able to do things, and that's okay. It's part of the process. And there is a process, an active process your child has some measure of control over. So, rather than general cheerleading—"You'll get it next time!"—involve your child in planning and problem-solving with prompts such as, "What do you think you should try next?"

6. Remind your child of the challenges they have overcome and improvements they have made in other areas. Moving from novice to pro is something your child has done over and over again.

7. Talk about what learning is like for you, or what it was like when you were younger. Be real with your child, acknowledging that making mistakes, struggling to grasp something, and losing are hard. Talk about what you do to keep yourself going.

8. Show your child that you value doing hard things on purpose. Routinely pose questions like, "What did you do today that made you think?" "What's a mistake you made today? What did you learn from it?" "What did you try even though it was hard?" "What's something you are working on?" "What do you want to get better at? How can you do that?" Encourage your child to ask you these questions, too. Then answer them in sincere and thoughtful ways.

9. Refer often to the 4 steps described in this book. Help your child practice making mistakes on purpose. Remind them to say their word, breathe, and use positive self-talk. These 4 steps will help your child carve a new brain path, one that will help them tolerate and move on from mistakes.

You can do this. Your child can do this. I'll be rooting for you.

Dr. Dawn

Resources

Organizations

These organizations provide information about childhood anxiety, and include therapist locators to assist with finding specialized care:

USA

The Anxiety and Depression Association of America:
https://adaa.org

The International OCD Foundation:
https://iocdf.org

UK

Anxiety UK:
www.anxietyuk.org.uk

Young Minds:
https://youngminds.org.uk

AU/NZ

Beyond Blue:
www.beyondblue.org.au

Kids Health:
https://kidshealth.org.nz

Please also reach out to your child's pediatrician for names of local providers.

Web-based resources

https://library.jkp.com
Dr. Dawn's Seven-Step Solution for When Worry Takes
Over: Easy-to-Implement Strategies for Parents or Carers of
Anxious Kids, see page 78.
Video Training Course

www.anxioustoddlers.com
Natasha Daniels of AT Parenting Survival creates podcasts, blog posts, and free resources about anxiety. She also offers subscription courses, coaching, and treatment.

https://childmind.org
This NY Institute offers articles on a host of topics, including anxiety, with a unique "Ask an Expert" feature providing trustworthy, relatable advice.

https://copingskillsforkids.com
Janine Halloran provides free, easy-to-implement, child-friendly tips on calming anxiety, managing stress, and more.

https://gozen.com
Kid-tested, therapist-approved, highly effective animated videos teaching skills related to anxiety, resilience, emotional intelligence, and more.

www.worrywisekids.org
Tamar Chansky of WorryWiseKids provides a treasure-trove of information for parents of anxious children.

Recommended reading

The books listed here are Dr. Dawn's current favorites, a snapshot from a particular moment in time. Please also search on your own, or check with your preferred bookseller, who can guide you toward up-to-date, appealing, effective books particularly suited to you and your child.

For younger children

Anxiety Relief Workbook for Kids: 40 Mindfulness, CBT, and ACT Activities to Find Peace from Anxiety and Worry by Agnes Selinger, PhD, Rockridge Press.

Hey Warrior: A Book for Kids about Anxiety by Karen Young, Little Steps Publishing.

Little Meerkat's Big Panic: A Story About Learning New Ways to Feel Calm by Jane Evans, Jessica Kingsley Publishers.

The Nervous Knight: A Story About Overcoming Worries and Anxiety by Anthony Lloyd Jones, Jessica Kingsley Publishers.

What to Do When You Worry Too Much: A Kid's Guide to Overcoming Anxiety by Dawn Huebner, PhD, American Psychological Association.

When Harley Has Anxiety: A Fun CBT Skills Activity Book to Help Manage Worries and Fears by Regine Galanti, PhD, Z Kids Publishing.

For older children

Coping Skills for Kids: Over 75 Coping Strategies to Help Kids Deal with Stress, Anxiety and Anger by Janine Halloran, PESI Publishing and Media.

Help! I've Got an Alarm Bell Going Off in My Head! How Panic, Anxiety and Stress Affect Your Body by K.L. Aspden, Jessica Kingsley Publishers.

My Anxiety Handbook by Sue Knowles, Bridie Gallagher, and Phoebe McEwen, Jessica Kingsley Publishers.

Name and Tame Your Anxiety: A Kid's Guide by Summer Batte, Free Spirit Publishing.

Outsmarting Worry: An Older Kid's Guide to Managing Anxiety by Dawn Huebner, PhD, Jessica Kingsley Publishers.

Superpowered: Transform Anxiety into Courage, Confidence, and Resilience by Renee Jain and Shefali Tsabary, PhD, Random House Books for Young Readers.

Take Control of OCD: A Kid's Guide to Conquering Anxiety and Managing OCD, 2nd Edition by Bonnie Zucker, PsyD, Routledge Press.

For parents

Anxious Kids, Anxious Parents: 7 Ways to Stop the Worry Cycle and Raise Courageous and Independent Children by Reid Wilson, PhD, and Lynn Lyons, LICSW, Health Communications Inc.

Breaking Free of Child Anxiety and OCD: A Scientifically Proven Program for Parents by Eli R. Lebowitz, PhD, Oxford University Press.

Freeing Your Child from Anxiety, Revised and Updated Edition: Practical Strategies to Overcome Fears, Worries, and Phobias and Be Prepared for Life by Tamar Chansky, PhD, Harmony.

Growing Up Mindful: Essential Practices to Help Children, Teens and Families Find Balance, Calm, and Resilience by Christopher Willard, PsyD, Sounds True.

Peaceful Parent, Happy Kids: How to Stop Yelling and Start Connecting by Laura Markham, PhD, TarcherPerigee.

The No Worries Guide to Raising Your Anxious Child: A Handbook to Help You and Your Anxious Child Thrive by Karen Lynn Cassiday, PhD, Jessica Kingsley Publishers.

The Yes Brain: How to Cultivate Courage, Curiosity and Resilience in Your Child by Dan Siegel, MD, and Tina Payne Bryson, PhD, Bantam Press.

Dr. Dawn's
SEVEN-STEP SOLUTION
FOR WHEN WORRY TAKES OVER

Easy-to-Implement Strategies for Parents or Carers of Anxious Kids

worry has a way of turning into WORRY in the blink of an eye. This upper-case WORRY causes children to fret about unlikely scenarios and shrink away from routine challenges, ultimately holding entire families hostage. But upper-case WORRY is predictable and manageable once you understand its tricks.

This 7-video series will help you recognize WORRY's tricks while teaching a handful of techniques to help you and your child break free.

Each video contains learning objectives and action steps along with need-to-know content presented in a clear, engaging manner by child psychologist and best-selling author, Dr. Dawn Huebner. The videos are available from https://library.jkp.com.

Video One: Trolling for Danger (time 8:15)

- The role of the amygdala in spotting and alerting us to danger
- What happens when the amygdala sets off an alarm
- Real dangers versus false alarms
- Calming the brain (yours and your child's) to get back to thinking

Video Two: The Worry Loop (time 10:15)

- The "loop" that keeps Worry in place
- How to identify where your child is in the Worry Loop

Video Three: Externalizing Anxiety (time 11:41)

- Externalizing anxiety as a powerful first step
- Talking back to Worry
- Teaching your child to talk back to Worry
- Talking back without entering into a debate

Video Four: Calming the Brain and Body (time 13:36)

- Breathing techniques
- Mindfulness techniques
- Distraction techniques
- Which technique (how to choose)?

Video Five: Getting Rid of Safety Behaviors (time 15:18)

- Preparation
- The role of exposure
- Explaining exposure to your child
- Creating an exposure hierarchy

Video Six: Worrying Less Is Not the Goal (time 13:02)

- The more you fight anxiety, the more it holds on
- The more you accommodate anxiety, the more it stays
- Anxiety is an error message, a false alarm
- When you stop letting Worry be in charge, it fades

Video Seven: Putting It All Together (time 19:42)

- A review of the main techniques
- Deciding where to start
- The role of rewards
- Supporting your child, not Worry